FOOD LOVERS

ITALIAN

RECIPES SELECTED BY MARIKA KUCEROVA

Trans
Atlantic
Press

All recipes serve four people, unless otherwise indicated.

For best results when cooking the recipes in this book, buy fresh ingredients and follow the instructions carefully. Make sure that everything is properly cooked through before serving, particularly any meat and shellfish, and note that as a general rule vulnerable groups such as the very young, elderly people, pregnant women, convalescents and anyone suffering from an illness should avoid dishes that contain raw or lightly cooked eggs.

For all recipes, quantities are given in standard U.S. cups and imperial measures, followed by the metric equivalent. Follow one set or the other, but not a mixture of both because conversions may not be exact. Standard spoon and cup measurements are level and are based on the following:

1 tsp. = 5 ml, 1 tbsp. = 15 ml, 1 cup = 250 ml / 8 fl oz.

Note that Australian standard tablespoons are 20 ml, so Australian readers should use 3 tsp. in place of 1 tbsp. when measuring small quantities.

The electric oven temperatures in this book are given for conventional ovens with top and bottom heat. When using a fan oven, the temperature should be decreased by about 20–40°F / 10–20°C – check the oven manufacturer's instruction book for further guidance. The cooking times given should be used as an approximate guideline only.

CONTENTS

ANTIPASTO OF MIXED VEGETABLES

Ingredients

2 zucchinis (courgettes)

2 eggplants (aubergines)

2 red bell peppers

2 white onions

2 tomatoes

2 garlic cloves

6 tbsp olive oil

1 sprig rosemary, chopped

Lemon wedges, for garnishing

Salt and freshly ground pepper

Method

Prep and cook time: 30 min plus 40 min standing time

1 Rinse the zucchinis (courgettes) and eggplants (aubergines). Remove the tops and stems. Slice lengthwise into ½ cm / ¼ inch thick slices.

2 Salt the eggplant slices and let stand for 30 minutes. Soak them in water for about 10 minutes to remove the salt.

3 Slice the bell peppers in half. Remove the ribs and seeds. Slice in half again.

4 Peel the onions and slice into wedges.

5 Rinse the tomatoes and cut out the stems. Slice in half.

6 Peel and finely chop the garlic and combine with the olive oil.

7 Pat the eggplant slices dry. Brush all the vegetables with oil.

8 Heat a ridged skillet or griddle pan and cook the vegetables in batches, turning frequently and brushing occasionally with the oil, until they are tender.

9 Arrange the vegetables on a platter. Remove the skin from the peppers if desired. Season with salt and pepper. Sprinkle with the rosemary and garnish with lemon wedges.

ASPARAGUS IN PROSCIUTTO

Ingredients

32 asparagus spears (about 900 g / 2 lb)

16 slices prosciutto

4 tbsp freshly grated Parmesan cheese

5 tbsp olive oil

2 handfuls arugula (rocket)

3 tbsp white wine vinegar

Salt and freshly ground pepper

Method

Prep and cook time: 35 min

1 Preheat the oven to 200C (400F / Gas Mark 6).

2 Peel the lower third of the asparagus spears and place the spears in boiling, salted water. Simmer gently for about 5 minutes, then drain, refresh in cold water and drain thoroughly.

3 Wrap each slice of prosciutto around 2 asparagus spears and lay side by side in an ovenproof baking dish. Sprinkle with a little freshly ground pepper.

4 Mix the Parmesan cheese with 3 tbsp olive oil and scatter over the asparagus. Bake in the oven for 6–8 minutes.

5 Wash the arugula (rocket), remove any hard stalks and arrange on plates. Drizzle with 2 tbsp olive oil and the vinegar. Sprinkle with salt and pepper and lay the asparagus on top. Serve immediately.

MINESTRONE SOUP

Ingredients

4 tomatoes

Olive oil

2 onions, finely chopped

2 carrots, finely diced

2 small zucchini (courgettes), finely diced

2 garlic cloves, peeled and crushed

250 g / 2 cups passata (sieved tomatoes)

750 ml / 2½ cups vegetable broth (stock)

600 g / 3 cups canned butter beans

Basil leaves, chopped

Freshly grated Parmesan cheese

Salt and freshly ground pepper

Wholewheat bread, to serve

Method
Prep and cook time: 35 min

1 Drop the tomatoes into boiling water for a few seconds, then skin, halve, deseed and finely dice.

2 Heat 2 tbsp oil in a pan and sweat the onions, carrots, zucchini (courgettes) and garlic over a low heat for 2–3 minutes, stirring.

3 Add the passata. Cook over a very low heat until reduced slightly, then add the broth (stock).

4 Bring to a boil, stir in the diced tomato and simmer over a low heat for about 10 minutes.

5 Stir in the drained beans and basil leaves and cook gently for a further 1 minute.

6 Season to taste with salt and pepper. Sprinkle with Parmesan cheese and serve with hearty wholewheat bread.

SPAGHETTI ALLA PUTTANESCA

Ingredients

100 g / 1 cup black olives, pitted

6 anchovy fillets

4 garlic cloves

2 dried chili peppers

3 tbsp olive oil

400 g / 2 cups canned tomatoes, chopped

450 g / 1 lb spaghetti

1 tbsp capers

Salt and freshly ground pepper

Method

Prep and cook time: 25 min

1 Coarsely chop the olives and the anchovies.

2 Peel and finely chop the garlic. Sauté in hot oil for about 2 minutes with the chili peppers and the anchovies.

3 Add the tomatoes and simmer gently for about 10 minutes.

4 Cook the spaghetti in well-salted boiling water until al dente.

5 Add the capers and olives to the sauce. Season with salt and pepper.

6 Combine the sauce with the well-drained spaghetti. Serve.

PIZZA MARGHERITA

Ingredients

For the base:

1½ tsp easy-bake yeast

¼ tsp sugar

450 g / 1 lb all-purpose (plain) flour

2 tbsp olive oil

1 tsp salt

For the topping:

4 tbsp olive oil, plus extra for drizzling

1 garlic clove, chopped

1 shallot, chopped

400 g / 2 cups canned tomatoes, chopped

2 tbsp tomato paste (purée)

1 tsp dried oregano

400 g / 2 cups mozzarella cheese

2 fresh tomatoes, sliced

2 tsp fresh oregano leaves

24 black olives

Salt and freshly ground pepper

Method

Prep and cook time: 45 min, plus I h resting time

1 Mix the yeast in a bowl with about ¹/₃ cup lukewarm water and the sugar.

2 Add the flour, olive oil and salt and knead to a pliable dough, adding a little water if the dough is too dry. Cover and put to rise in a warm place for about 1 hour.

3 Preheat the oven to 220C (425F / Gas Mark 7).

4 Heat the oil in a pan and sauté the garlic and shallot until translucent.

5 Add the canned tomatoes and tomato paste (purée) and stew gently for about 20 minutes. Season with oregano, salt and pepper.

6 Divide the dough into 4 and roll out on a lightly floured surface into circles of approximately 22 cm / 9 inch diameter, leaving the edges a little thicker.

7 Put the pizza bases on 2 greased cookie sheets and spread with the tomato sauce. Slice the mozzarella thinly and lay on the pizzas. Drizzle with a little olive oil.

8 Bake in the preheated oven for about 20 minutes. Take out and top with fresh tomato slices, oregano and olives.

RED MULLET
WITH BEANS AND TOMATOES

Ingredients

450 g / 1 lb fava (broad) beans

Handful of basil leaves

3 tomatoes

8 red mullet fillets, with skin

2 tbsp butter

1 garlic clove

3 tbsp olive oil

5 tbsp fish broth (stock)

Cayenne pepper

2 tsp white wine vinegar

Salt and freshly ground pepper

Method

Prep and cook time: 25 min

1 Remove the beans from the pods and cook in boiling water for 10 minutes. Refresh in cold water and slip the beans out of their skins.

2 Rinse the basil and shake dry. Remove the leaves from the stems and slice into strips, reserving a few whole leaves to garnish.

3 Blanch the tomatoes for a few seconds. Immerse in cold water. Remove the skins, quarter and deseed. Chop and season lightly with salt and pepper.

4 Rinse the fish fillets under cold water and pat dry.

5 Heat 1 tbsp butter in a large skillet. Fry the fillets for about 4 minutes each side. Arrange on 4 warmed plates, skin side up.

6 Swirl the chopped tomatoes around the skillet with the remaining butter. Add the beans, fish broth (stock) and basil strips. Combine well and pour over the fillets.

7 Peel and crush the garlic. Mix with the oil, cayenne pepper and vinegar and season to taste. Drizzle over the fish fillets.

8 Garnish with the reserved basil leaves and serve lukewarm.

SPAGHETTI WITH CLAMS AND SQUID

Ingredients

400 g / 1 lb small squid, cleaned and ready to cook

400 g / 1 lb clams

1 lemon

2 cloves garlic

100 ml / 7 tbsp white wine

400 g / 1 lb spaghetti

1 leek

4 tbsp olive oil

4 tsp white vermouth

Method

Prep and cook time: 35 min

1 Rinse, drain and coarsely chop the squid. Discard any clams that are open.

2 Rinse the lemon under hot water. Remove the zest and squeeze out the juice.

3 Peel the garlic and slice.

4 Bring the wine, half of the lemon juice and 100 ml / ½ cup of water to boil in a pan. Put the clams in the pan and cover. Simmer for about 8 minutes or until the clams open. Discard any unopened clams.

5 Cook the spaghetti according to the package instructions.

6 Remove the roots and trim the ragged ends of the leek. Slice the white and bright green parts on a diagonal into rings.

7 Sauté the squid in 4 tbsp of oil for about 2 minutes. Add the leek and the sliced garlic. Continue to sauté for another 2–3 minutes.

8 Pour in the vermouth and the remainder of the lemon juice. Simmer briefly.

9 Toss everything together with the well drained spaghetti (and a little of the pasta water). Season with salt and pepper.

BAKED POLENTA GNOCCHI

Ingredients

250 g / 1¼ cups quick-cooking polenta

For the sauce:

4 tbsp olive oil

1 onion, chopped

1 garlic clove, chopped

450 g / 1 lb ripe tomatoes

1 tbsp basil, shredded

70 g / ⅓ cup butter

50 g / ½ cup freshly grated Parmesan cheese

Salt and freshly ground pepper

Method

Prep and cook time: 50 min

1 Prepare the polenta according to the package instructions.

2 Heat the olive oil and sweat the onion and garlic until soft.

3 Blanch the tomatoes briefly, refresh in cold water, then skin, quarter, deseed and dice finely.

4 Add to the onion with salt and pepper and simmer for 2–3 minutes. Stir in the basil.

5 Preheat the oven to 200C (400F / Gas Mark 6).

6 Butter an ovenproof dish.

7 Using a moistened tablespoon, cut gnocchi out of the polenta and arrange in the dish.

8 Pour the tomato sauce over, sprinkle with grated Parmesan cheese and dot with the remaining butter.

9 Bake in the preheated oven for 25–30 minutes.

SPINACH CANNELLONI

Ingredients

Olive oil, for greasing

250 g / 9 oz cannelloni tubes
(no pre-cook type)

For the filling:

500 g / 6 cups spinach

200 g / 2 cups ricotta cheese

1 egg

Nutmeg

Salt and freshly ground pepper

For the tomatoes:

225 g / ½ lb tomatoes

1 shallot

1 garlic clove

1 tbsp olive oil

For the béchamel sauce:

1 tbsp butter

1 tbsp flour

250 ml / 1 cup milk

75 g / ¾ cup freshly grated
Parmesan cheese

Salt and freshly ground pepper

Method

Prep and cook time: 1 h

1 Lightly grease an ovenproof dish with a little olive oil.
Preheat the oven to 200C (400F / Gas Mark 6).

2 Wash the spinach well, put into a pan dripping wet
and heat over a medium heat until it wilts. Drain, refresh
in cold water, drain again and squeeze out excess water.

3 Roughly chop the spinach and mix with the mashed
ricotta. Stir in the egg and season with salt, pepper and
nutmeg.

4 Spoon the mixture into the cannelloni tubes and
place them side by side in the baking dish.

5 Drop the tomatoes into boiling water for a few
seconds, refresh in cold water, then skin, quarter,
deseed and chop roughly.

6 Peel and finely chop the shallot and garlic. Heat
the oil and sauté the shallot and garlic then add the
tomatoes and cook over a medium heat for about
5 minutes.

7 For the béchamel sauce, melt the butter, stir in
the flour and cook for a couple of minutes without
browning. Then gradually stir in the milk. Simmer for
10 minutes, season with salt and pepper and stir in half
of the Parmesan.

8 Spread the tomatoes on the cannelloni. Pour the
sauce over and sprinkle with the rest of the Parmesan
cheese. Dot with butter and bake for about 30 minutes.

MARINATED VEGETABLES WITH SAUSAGE

Ingredients

12 small artichokes

1 lemon

2 garlic cloves

225 g / ½ lb salsiccia (fresh Italian sausage)

225 g / ½ lb mushrooms

4 red bell peppers

About 160 ml / ⅔ cup olive oil

3 sprigs rosemary

50 g / ½ cup green olives, pitted

50 g / ½ cup black olives, pitted

20 g / 1 tbsp capers

Freshly ground pepper

Method

Prep and cook time: 40 min
Marinating time: at least 2 h

1 Rinse, clean and remove the tips (the upper $\frac{1}{3}$) of the artichokes. Remove the tough outer leaves. Remove the stem, the lower portion of the hard bottom and any fibers.

2 Squeeze the juice from the lemon. Pour some lemon juice over the artichokes (this prevents them from darkening).

3 Boil the artichokes in salted water for 8 minutes. Drain and allow to cool until lukewarm.

4 Peel the garlic cloves.

5 Cut the salsiccia into slices.

6 Clean the mushrooms. Slice any large ones in half.

7 Slice the bell peppers in half. Remove the ribs and seeds. Slice into wide strips.

8 Sauté the sausage pieces in 2 tbsp of hot oil. Put them in a flat dish.

9 Add the remaining lemon juice, garlic cloves, mushrooms, artichokes, peppers, rosemary, olives, capers and remaining olive oil. Season with pepper and mix together thoroughly. Allow to sit for at least 2 hours before serving.

LEMON RISOTTO WITH HERBS AND PINE NUTS

Ingredients

About 1 liter / 4 cups chicken broth (stock)

1 onion, peeled and finely chopped

2 garlic cloves, peeled and finely chopped

3 tbsp olive oil

400 g / 2 cups risotto rice

250 ml / 1 cup dry white wine

1 lemon, juice and zest

1 tbsp chopped fresh parsley leaves

3 tbsp pine nuts

3 tbsp freshly grated Parmesan cheese

1 tbsp butter

Lemon halves, for garnishing

Salt and freshly ground pepper

Method

Prep and cook time: 30 min

1 Heat the broth (stock) in a pan.

2 Sauté the onion and garlic in a skillet with 3 tbsp of hot oil.

3 Add the rice and sauté briefly. Pour in the wine. Bring the ingredients to a boil quickly then add the lemon juice and zest and a little hot broth.

4 Cook the risotto over medium heat, stirring constantly and adding more broth gradually as it is absorbed, until the rice is creamy but still firm (about 20 minutes).

5 Mix the parsley, pine nuts, Parmesan cheese and butter into the risotto. Season to taste with salt and pepper. Garnish with the lemon halves and serve.

CHICKEN WITH CAPONATA

Ingredients

4 chicken legs

8 sage leaves

2 garlic cloves, chopped

2 red chili peppers, deseeded and chopped

4 tbsp olive oil

2 tbsp lemon juice

For the caponata:

1 medium eggplant (aubergine)

1 celery stalk

4 tomatoes

2 tbsp olive oil

1 yellow bell pepper, deseeded and sliced

1 onion, sliced

50 g / ½ cup pitted black olives

1 tbsp capers

White wine vinegar

Salt and freshly ground pepper.

Method

Prep and cook time: 1 h 10 min

1 Preheat the oven to 180C (350F / Gas Mark 4).

2 Take the chicken legs and separate the drumstick from the thigh at the joint. Put one sage leaf under the skin of each piece of chicken.

3 Mix together the garlic, chili pepper, olive oil and lemon juice. Rub into the chicken and put in a roasting pan.

4 Bake the chicken in the preheated oven for about 40 minutes until golden brown.

5 Coarsely chop the eggplant (aubergine).

6 Reserve the celery stalk leaves for garnish. Slice the rest.

7 Blanch the tomatoes, immerse in cold water and remove the skins. Slice into quarters and remove the seeds.

8 Sauté the eggplant in hot oil until lightly browned.

9 Add the bell pepper, onion and sliced celery. Season with salt and pepper. Cook, covered, for about 10 minutes stirring occasionally.

10 Add the tomatoes, olives and capers. Cook, uncovered, for about 4 minutes more. Season to taste with the vinegar, salt and pepper.

11 Divide the vegetables among the plates and arrange the chicken pieces on top. Garnish with the reserved celery leaves and serve.

TOMATO AND MOZZARELLA LASAGNA

Ingredients

Olive oil, for greasing

2 garlic cloves, finely chopped

400 g / 2 cups canned tomatoes, chopped

2 sprigs basil

350 g / ¾ lb mozzarella cheese

12 lasagna sheets, no-precook type

75 g / ¾ cup Parmesan cheese

Salt and freshly ground pepper

For the béchamel sauce:

50 g / ¼ cup butter

3 tbsp flour

About 500 ml / 2 cups milk

Salt and freshly ground pepper

Method

Prep and cook time: 1 h 20 min

1 Lightly grease an ovenproof dish with a little olive oil. Preheat the oven to 180C (350 F / Gas Mark 4).

2 Combine the garlic with the tomatoes. Season with salt and pepper.

3 Remove the basil leaves from the stems, chop the leaves and stir into the tomatoes.

4 Slice the mozzarella and reserve a few slices.

5 For the béchamel sauce, melt the butter in a pan, stir in the flour and cook briefly. Add the milk gradually while stirring. Simmer for about 10 minutes, stirring continuously. Season with salt and pepper.

6 Spoon a little of the béchamel sauce into the bottom of the baking dish.

7 Place a layer of lasagna sheets on top, then some of the tomato mixture and another layer of lasagna. Add some more béchamel sauce, some mozzarella and a few basil leaves.

8 Continue layering until all the ingredients have been used. Finish with béchamel sauce and the reserved mozzarella.

9 Sprinkle with the Parmesan cheese and season with salt and pepper.

10 Bake in the preheated oven for 40–45 minutes until golden brown.

SALMON WITH MOZZARELLA, TOMATOES AND BASIL

Ingredients

For the salad:

400 g / 2 cups mozzarella cheese

4 tomatoes

1 tbsp pumpkin seed oil

1 tbsp olive oil

3 tbsp white balsamic vinegar

Salt and freshly ground pepper

For the fish:

1 slice melba toast

30 g / 1 cup basil leaves

2 tbsp pine nuts

2 tbsp freshly grated Parmesan cheese

1 egg yolk

About 4 tbsp olive oil

675 g / 1½ lb salmon fillet

Salt and freshly ground pepper

Basil, for garnishing

Method

Prep and cook time: 40 min

1 Slice the mozzarella into 8 pieces. Divide among four deep plates.

2 Rinse the tomatoes, cut out the cores and slice. Decorate each plate with tomato slices. Season lightly with salt and pepper.

3 Mix the oils with the balsamic vinegar. Drizzle over the salad and allow to marinate.

4 Remove the crust from the melba toast. Break the bread into crumbs.

5 Put the bread crumbs, basil leaves, pine nuts, Parmesan cheese, egg yolk and about 2 tbsp of olive oil in a food processor. Purée into a paste.

6 Rinse the salmon and pat dry. Slice into 4 pieces.

7 Slice a little pocket into the sides of each piece of fish with a knife and fill with the paste.

8 Gently sauté the fish in hot oil for 3–4 minutes on each side, until golden brown. Season with salt and pepper. Cut in half and arrange on top of the salad. Garnish with the fresh basil and serve.

POTATO AND TOMATO SALAD WITH PESTO DRESSING

Ingredients

900 g / 2 lb small, new potatoes

675 g / 1½ lb small tomatoes

For the pesto:

4 sprigs fresh basil

2 sprigs fresh parsley

2 garlic cloves

50 g / ½ cup pine nuts

50 g / ½ cup Parmesan cheese

About 7 tbsp olive oil

3 tbsp lemon juice

Salt and freshly ground pepper

8 slices prosciutto, to serve

Method

Prep and cook time: 40 min

1 Boil the potatoes in well-salted water for about 25 minutes until you can pierce them easily with a fork.

2 Cut the tomatoes in half.

3 Remove the basil and parsley leaves from the stems. Put the herbs along with the peeled garlic, pine nuts and Parmesan into a food processor. Chop coarsely. Gradually add enough olive oil to make a thin paste. Season with the lemon juice, salt and pepper.

4 Drain the potatoes and allow some of the excess water to evaporate. Slice in half and gently mix with the tomatoes and pesto dressing.

5 Arrange on plates with the prosciutto and serve.

LAMB CHOPS
WITH PESTO

Ingredients

40 g / 2 cups basil leaves

2 garlic cloves, peeled

1 tbsp pine nuts

Olive oil

2 handfuls arugula (rocket)

8 lamb chops

Salt and freshly ground pepper

Method

Prep and cook time: 25 min

1 For the pesto, pick off the basil leaves and purée with the peeled garlic, pine nuts and sufficient oil to produce a creamy mixture, adding the oil in a steady stream. Season to taste with salt and pepper.

2 Arrange the arugula (rocket) on plates.

3 Wash and dry the chops and season with salt and pepper.

4 Heat a little oil and fry the chops for 2–3 minutes on each side, or until golden brown.

5 Place two lamb chops on each plate and serve drizzled with pesto.

RIBBON NOODLES WITH LAMB RAGOUT

Ingredients

3 tbsp olive oil

900 g / 2 lb lamb, cut into bite-size pieces

2 onions, chopped

2 garlic cloves, chopped

1 tbsp tomato paste (purée)

100 ml / 7 tbsp dry red wine

250 ml / 1 cup beef broth (stock)

400 g / 2 cups canned tomatoes, chopped

1 sprig rosemary

1 bay leaf

450 g / 1 lb pappardelle

Salt and freshly ground pepper

Fresh rosemary, for garnishing

Method

Prep and cook time: 1 h 20 min

1 Heat the oil in a large pan and sear the meat until brown all over

2 Add the onions, garlic and tomato paste (purée) and continue to fry for 2 minutes more.

3 Pour in the red wine. Simmer briefly.

4 Add the broth (stock) and the tomatoes, bring to a boil and season with salt and pepper.

5 Add the sprig of rosemary and the bay leaf to the sauce. Simmer gently for about 1 hour, stirring occasionally. Add a little water to the sauce if needed.

6 Cook the noodles in well-salted boiling water until al dente.

7 Remove the rosemary and the bay leaf from the ragout. Season to taste with salt and pepper.

8 Drain the pasta and divide among 4 plates. Pour the ragout over the top and garnish with the fresh rosemary.

PENNE
WITH WHITE BEANS
AND PESTO

Ingredients

450 g / 1 lb penne

250 g / 1¼ cups canned white beans

20 g / 1 cup fresh basil leaves

20 g / 1 cup arugula (rocket)

1 sprig parsley

1 garlic clove

50 g / ½ cup pine nuts

About 3 tbsp olive oil

1 lemon

25 g / ¼ cup Parmesan cheese

Salt and freshly ground pepper

Method

Prep and cook time: 20 min

1 Boil the penne in salted water until al dente.

2 Put the beans in a sieve. Rinse and drain.

3 Rinse the basil, arugula (rocket) and parsley leaves and shake dry. Discard any discolored leaves and put all the rest of the leaves in a food processor.

4 Peel the garlic clove and add it to the herbs along with the pine nuts. Pour in the olive oil and 1–2 tbsp of the penne cooking water. Purée until smooth.

5 Remove the zest from the lemon. Squeeze out the juice. Season the pesto with the lemon juice, salt and pepper.

6 Put the beans in with the penne during the last 2 minutes of cooking time. Drain.

7 Combine the pesto with the beans and penne. Divide among the plates. Sprinkle with the lemon zest and Parmesan cheese. Serve.

SARDINES WITH TOMATO AND EGG VINAIGRETTE

Ingredients

24 fresh sardines (ready to cook, deboned, heads removed)

Flour, for dredging

8 tbsp olive oil

3 tomatoes

2 eggs

3 tbsp balsamic vinegar

2½ tsp sugar

1 radicchio lettuce

Salt and freshly ground pepper

Fresh basil leaves, to garnish

Method

Prep and cook time: 30 min

1 Rinse the sardines well under cold water. Pat dry.

2 Dredge the sardines in the flour. Sauté on both sides in 2 tbsp of hot oil for about 3 minutes until golden brown. Season with salt and pepper. Remove from the pan. Allow to drain on paper towels.

3 Blanch the tomatoes for a few seconds. Refresh in cold water. Remove the skins and cut into quarters. Remove the seeds and finely chop.

4 Hard boil the eggs. Refresh in cold water. Peel and chop. Mix with the balsamic vinegar and the remaining olive oil. Add the tomatoes. Season with salt, pepper and sugar.

5 Remove the core from the radicchio. Slice into 1 cm / ½ inch wide pieces.

6 Divide the radicchio and sardines among the plates. Pour the tomato and egg vinaigrette over the top. Garnish with the basil. Serve lukewarm or cold.

TORTA DELLA NONNA

Ingredients

For the dough:

300 g / 3 cups flour

1 egg yolk

1 egg

200 g / 1 cup butter, flaked

100 g / ²/₃ cup ground almonds

2½ tsp salt

50 g / ¼ cup sugar

For the filling:

400 ml / 1²/₃ cups milk

1 tsp vanilla extract

4 egg yolks

50 g / ¼ cup sugar

2 tbsp corn starch (cornflour), mixed with a little water

½ tsp lemon zest

50 g / ½ cup pine nuts

Confectioners' (icing) sugar, for dusting

Method

Prep and cook time: 1 h plus 30 min resting time

1 Mound the flour on a work surface. Make a well in the middle and put in the egg yolk, egg and flaked butter.

2 Add the almonds, salt and sugar. Working from the middle, knead into a smooth dough. Wrap in plastic wrap and chill for about 30 minutes.

3 To make the filling, bring the milk and the vanilla extract to a boil while stirring. Stir in the egg yolk, sugar and lemon zest and add the corn starch (cornflour). Cook while stirring continuously until creamy.

4 Pour the creamy mixture through a sieve into a bowl and allow to cool to room temperature.

5 Preheat the oven to 180C (350 F / Gas Mark 4).

6 Roll out the dough. Use it to line a 26 cm / 10 inch springform pan, the dough coming 3 cm / 1½ inches above the top of the pan. Prick the crust all over with a fork.

7 Pour the filling over the crust and smooth. Sprinkle with the pine nuts and fold the edges of the dough over the filling.

8 Bake in the preheated oven for about 40 minutes until golden brown. Allow to cool slightly then remove the sides of the pan. Cool to room temperature on a wire rack. Dust with confectioners' (icing) sugar and serve.

CAFFÈ LATTE ICE CREAM

Ingredients

2 eggs

70 g / ⅓ cup sugar

150 ml / ⅔ cup milk

150 ml / ⅔ cup espresso

200 ml / scant cup whipping cream

100 g / 1 cup chopped dark chocolate, 70% cocoa solids

To decorate:

100 ml / 7 tbsp milk

Mint leaves

1 cup raspberries

Method

Prep and cook time: 25 min plus 4h freezing time

1 Whisk together the eggs, sugar, milk and espresso in a large bowl set over a pan of simmering water until the mixture is thick and creamy.

2 Let the mixture cool, stirring from time to time.

3 Whip the cream until stiff peaks form. Fold the cream and chocolate into the cold egg mixture.

4 Put the mixture to churn in an ice cream machine, or pour into a flat metal dish and freeze for at least 4 hours, stirring well every 30 minutes.

5 To serve, use a scoop to put the ice cream into dessert glasses. Pour chilled milk over the top, garnish with mint and decorate with the raspberries.

TIRAMISÙ

Ingredients

5 egg yolks

50 g / ½ cup confectioners' (icing) sugar

500 g / 2 cups mascarpone

3 tbsp almond liqueur

500 ml / 2 cups strong espresso

16 lady fingers (sponge fingers)

Cocoa powder, for dusting

Confectioners' (icing) sugar, for dusting

Method

Prep and cook time: 30 min

1 Beat the egg yolks and confectioners' (icing) sugar until foaming, then stir in the mascarpone and the liqueur.

2 Put the espresso in a flat dish, dip half of the sponge fingers in the espresso and lay them on the base of a rectangular serving dish.

3 Spread with half of the egg/cream mixture and dust with cocoa. Repeat the process with the remaining sponge fingers and mascarpone cream. Dust with cocoa and confectioners' sugar before serving.

Published by Transatlantic Press

First published in 2011

Transatlantic Press
38 Copthorne Road, Croxley Green, Hertfordshire WD3 4AQ

© Transatlantic Press

Images and Recipes by StockFood © The Food Image Agency

Recipes selected by Marika Kucerova, StockFood

A catalogue record for this book is available from the British Library.

ISBN 978-1-908533-61-6

Printed in China